Teacher's Manual

# Just Writing:

# Grammar, Punctuation, and Style for the Legal Writer

**Second Edition**

**Anne Enquist**
**Laurel Currie Oates**

**ASPEN**
PUBLISHERS

111 Eighth Avenue, New York, NY 10011
www.aspenpublishers.com

ISBN  0 – 7355 – 4956 – 7

This manual is made available as a courtesy to law teachers with the understanding that it will not be reproduced, quoted or cited, except as where indicated.  In the event that anyone would like to cite the manual for thoughts drawn from it, a reference to the relevant page number of the materials text (with the formula "suggested by") may be appropriate.

Copies of this manual are available on computer diskette.  Teachers who have adopted the casebook may obtain a copy of the diskette, free of charge, by calling the Aspen Publishers sales assistant at 1 – 800 – 950 – 5259.

Permissions
Aspen Publishers
111 Eighth Avenue
New York, NY 10011

1  2  3  4  5

# Table of Contents

## *The Teaching Materials Website*

Legal writing professors who have adopted *Just Writing* for one or more of their legal writing courses can use the Teaching Materials Website:

www.aspenlawschool.com/oatesandenquist/teachingandtesting materials/.

This website integrates the materials found in this Teacher's Manual with a wide variety of additional materials for teaching, such as the following:

- Introductions to teaching various topics
- Lesson plans
- Sample handouts and Powerpoint presentations
- Sample memoranda, briefs, and client letters
- Sample exams
- Quick Tips about writing

In addition, new teaching materials are frequently added to the website.

If you would like to examine the Teaching Materials Website, please contact Aspen Publishers using the information below and a Sales Associate will provide you with a username and password to access the materials on the website. Aspen will also provide technical support if you have trouble accessing the site.

Aspen Publishers
Phone:  800-950-5259
Fax: 617-349-1692
legaledu@aspenpublishers.com

## The Electronic Diagnostic Test
## For Grammar and Punctuation

Legal writing professors who have adopted *Just Writing* for one or more of their legal writing courses can use the Electronic Diagnostic Test to test their students' grammar and punctuation skills. The Electronic Diagnostic Test can be found at the following website: www.aspenlawschool.com/diagnostictest/.

The Electronic Diagnostic Test has the following features:

- It grades itself
- Students receive the results and can email them to their professor
- Students can review annotated answers that are keyed to *Just Writing*
- Students also receive a Pattern of Errors sheet that identifies gaps in their grammar and punctuation background

If you would like to examine the Electronic Diagnostic Test, please contact Aspen Publishers using the information below and a Sales Associate will provide you with a username and password to access the test. Aspen will also provide technical support if you or your students have trouble accessing the site.

Aspen Publishers
Phone: 800-950-5259
Fax: 617-349-1692
legaledu@aspenpublishers.com

# *Writing Exercises*

When students purchase a copy of the second edition of *Just Writing*, they receive a CD with Writing Exercises and the answers to those exercises. These exercises are intended to reinforce points about writing in the text and give the students an opportunity to practice what they have learned. You may find that it is helpful to assign a given exercise to all of your students or to only those students having difficulty with a certain writing point, rule, or concept.

The following is a list of the topics covered in the exercises, the pages numbers where the exercise and its answer appears on the CD, and the point at what you may wish to assign a given exercise. Note that there are no exercises for Chapters 1, 2, 7, and 10.

# *Using Student Work in Class*

Throughout these the Teaching Notes, we recommend using student samples to demonstrate how to apply what is being taught in the text to the students' current writing assignment. Done well, this teaching method is potentially one of the most powerful at the legal writing professor's disposal.

Although the ideal and probably most effective teaching method would be to give each student individualized feedback on each draft of each paper, that level of one-on-one teaching is not possible in most legal writing programs. Working as a group through a <u>carefully selected</u> student sample is a practical compromise. Although some students may still need an individual conference about their own paper, most will be able to transfer the points made in the class discussion of the sample to their own writing.

## A. Rationale for the Method

The hardest thing to teach in legal writing is decision-making and judgment. When a class works together on a student sample, students learn just that: they observe not just the decisions the writer made to create the draft but also those being made by their professor and fellow students as they attempt to critique and revise it. They see several other legal writers in the process of making choices about writing. They see them, and themselves, articulating the rationale underlying those choices, weighing the merits of several options, and balancing several writing concerns against each other. In short, such classes are often the closest thing we have to teaching students how to write.

Classes that use student samples also raise students' awareness of their readers. They hear how different readers react to a piece of writing. They hear where readers are confused, as well as where they are persuaded.

Using student drafts in class is effective for other reasons as well. For example, students see classes that use student samples as immediately relevant to their own learning. Because the students are currently grappling with the same or similar writing challenges in their own drafts, they are ready, often eager, to work through and think about the questions and issues a representative sample raises. Put another way, people learn best when they need to know something; writing a draft for the assignment generates a "need to know" that can be fulfilled by a discussion about a representative sample.

## B. Logistics of Using Student Samples

Classes that use a student sample as the text for the class work best when the students have completed a draft of an assignment and are now about to start revising that draft. For this reason, have the students turn in or email a copy of their drafts a day or at least several hours before the class so that you can read through a fair number of them, determine what points you want the class to focus on, select an example that demonstrates one or more of those points, <u>remove the student's name</u>, and then photocopy or make a transparency (or both) of the example. If you have access to a document reader, you can simply use the hard copy of the example.

(At most law schools, first-year students are assigned to sections. Having the drafts due right before their section's first class of the day works reasonably well if you can clear your calendar so that the hours before your legal writing class can be spent skimming or reading the drafts, selecting a sample, and having photocopies made. It is a tight turnaround, but many find the relevance of the resulting classes well worth the added time pressure.)

Notice the strong recommendation to remove the student's name before photocopying or making a transparency of his or her paper. For most students, having their paper selected as the example used in class is initially intimidating. (Ultimately, many find it to be a great advantage to have their work selected. You may want to point out these advantages to the class.) The initial intimidation can be minimized, however, by allowing, indeed encouraging, the student to remain anonymous.

Because it is intimidating for students to have their writing under scrutiny even when names have been removed from the papers, remind the class that the example is a draft written by one of their peers. As the leader of the discussion, set a collaborative tone and model constructive criticism. Be sure to point out what was done well in the student sample, as well as what needs to be changed. Resist the temptation to ridicule the writing, and prohibit class members from getting carried away in their criticism.

Legal writing professors who are teaching more than one section of the same class have yet another way of minimizing the problem of a student feeling uncomfortable about having his or her paper used as a sample for class discussion. Simply make it a practice to use examples from one class when teaching the other and vice versa.

## C. Criteria for Selecting a Student Sample

Because student samples that you choose become the primary text for that class, it is critical that the samples be well chosen. Usually it is best to select strong but not perfect examples and ones that demonstrate only one or two problems. (When the examples have too many problems, the class discussion tends to become unfocused. In addition, the student whose paper is being used may become overwhelmed by the recommendations.)

As you read through the papers, have in mind what points you want to emphasize in the class and thus be looking for papers that will generate the desired discussion. You may also want to look for common problems and then select samples that demonstrate those problems.

You may find that you need to modify or clean up samples before using them in class. As long as you tell the class that you have modified the example, you can correct errors that may distract the class, or you may want to add in or exaggerate errors to help make a point.

Whenever possible, use more than one example. If you use only one, it implies that there is only one right way of doing something. If you use two samples, you can contrast the techniques, having students explore why one might be more effective than the other.

## D. Teaching Recommendations

1. Before using student samples, explain to the class members the rationale for using their own work as examples.

2. Remind students not to identify themselves as the author of a particular sample.

3. Keep the focus on the paper that is being critiqued and on the points you want to raise in that paper. Discourage students from talking or asking about what they did in their own paper.

4. Teach decision-making within the rhetorical situation by asking questions.

5. Does the statement of facts give the attorney the information that he or she needs? After reading the statement of facts, will an attorney not familiar with the case understand what happened? How will an attorney respond to the writing style? How could this sentence or paragraph be rewritten?

6. End by summarizing the discussion. What did the author do well? What does the author need to work on?

## A Final Concern about Using Student Samples in Class

In addition to the concerns that have already been addressed, some legal writing professors are concerned that using student samples leads to copying the student sample. This problem can be prevented in several ways, the easiest of which is to collect the photocopies of the sample before the end of class. You may also want to point out that while you have selected a strong example, the example still needs work. You will also want to use excerpts from student papers and not photocopy or make transparencies of entire papers.

# *Using Document Readers, Power Point, and Overhead Projectors in Class*

## A.    Document Readers

Throughout the *Teaching Notes,* we frequently recommend using samples of student work Undoubtedly the easiest was to use student samples is with a document reader. They allow you to project on a screen exactly what is on the hard copy.  If your school does not have document readers, start lobbying your dean now to get them.

## B.    PowerPoint

PowerPoint programs can be used to create polished presentations about a variety of topics.  The main advantage of PowerPoint is its dynamic graphic capability.  It can bring some pizzazz to an otherwise dull topic.  Used with discretion, for example, PowerPoint can enliven a class about a topic like citation, but a warning is also in order: PowerPoint presentations can lull students into a rather passive mode.

To use PowerPoint presentations to best effect, use a remote mouse so that you are not tied to the keyboard. Laser pointers also work well with PowerPoint presentations because they do not block the projection.

## C.    Overhead Projectors

If your school has not yet acquired document readers, another way to use student samples is with transparencies on an overhead projector. Ideally, students would have the transparency projected up on the screen to look at, as well as a photocopied version in hand. The transparency allows the professor to highlight points and write in revisions right on the page for all to see; the photocopied version gives the student a more legible copy on which to make his or her own notes. The key, of course, is to know when to use what, depending upon what you want the students to focus on.

Transparencies can be made in at least two ways: you can write by hand directly on the transparency, or you can use the feature on most photocopiers that allows you to make transparencies of a printed page. (For example, on Xerox 5042 photocopiers, select the "paper tray bypass" feature, place a blank transparency in the appropriate bypass slot, and place the printed page on the glass under the cover.) One particularly effective use of transparencies combines both printed and handwritten words on the same transparency to demonstrate revising, for example, or any number of other writing skills.

Using transparencies and an overhead projector is quite simple and effective if you remember a few tips.

1.    You can enlarge the size of the type in several ways:

   a.    use the enlarge feature on your photocopier before you make the transparency,

   b.    move the overhead projector further away from the screen and then refocus it.

2.    You can focus the students' attention on a specific part of the transparency by simply putting a blank sheet of paper over all but the part you wish to focus on.

3.    You can highlight certain points with a transparency pen. You may want to use a washable rather than permanent pen if the same transparency will be used again.

4.    You can highlight certain features, such as transitions or citations, by making an overlay transparency.

5.    When using an overhead projector or any other audiovisual equipment, be prepared for technical problems. Checking out the location of the electric outlet and the availability of extension cords and extra bulbs for the overhead can save precious class time.

6.    When students are asked to write on transparencies, be sure you have supplied them with washable rather than permanent markers. A drop of water on a tissue makes a handy "eraser" when washable markers have been used.

7.    When using a series of transparencies, consider numbering them in an inconspicuous corner. Insert a blank sheet of paper between transparencies to prevent smearing and to allow easy reading in hand.

8.    Transparency pens dry out quickly if left uncapped. Bring extras with you to class.

Transparencies also have a few disadvantages that you will want to keep in mind. We have already alluded to the problem of students being able to read off the transparency because of the size of the print. You will also have to plan where to project the transparency so that the screen (or wall) is comfortably visible from where all the students sit. Also keep in mind that almost all overhead projectors light up a transparency area that is slightly smaller than a standard 8 1/2 X 11 page and that the machines are designed for the standard, vertical rectangle of a typed page, not the horizontal layout of a flow chart.

One asset of overhead projectors--that the professor can face the class while reading off the transparency--has the accompanying drawback that the professor may be trying to read from a glary surface. This drawback can be minimized, however, by using transparencies with a lightly colored background.

Undoubtedly the key assets of transparencies are that they allow professors to have material pre-written (so no class time is lost while it is written on the board) and that they give professors an effective way to return to earlier points. For example, a group of students that has recorded its work on a transparency can quickly present its work at a subsequent class by simply starting with what they have on the transparency. A transparency of a sample from a paper used to demonstrate one point on Tuesday can be reused for another point on Thursday and then used again the next week to review both points. Transparencies of graphics can be used whenever relevant to remind students of what part of a total concept they are now focusing on.

Tuesday:

**audience**                                   purpose

                    rhetorical
                    situation

writer                                         conventions

Thursday :

audience                                       **purpose**

                    rhetorical
                    situation

writer                                         conventions

In addition, graphics on transparencies can be added to and developed as needed.

Original Transparency:

### COMPOSING PROCESS OF A LEGAL MEMORANDUM

---

prewriting            drafting            revising

Original Transparency Plus Additions:

### COMPOSING PROCESS OF A LEGAL MEMORANDUM

| prewriting | drafting | revising |
|---|---|---|
| depositions | outline/plan | edit |
| research | rough draft | |
| theory of case | second draft | proofread |

Like any other classroom tool, though, document readers, Powerpoints, and transparencies and overhead projectors are no panacea of teaching. They should be used thoughtfully and not as a gimmick. They are effective only when they further the teaching objective.

# Commenting on and Critiquing Law Students' Writing

Few, if any, parts of the legal writing professor's job are more important than critiquing law students' writing. In this very individualized form of instruction, students learn whether or not they have been able to apply what they have read in their textbook and what was taught in the legal writing class to their own research, analysis, and writing. Here, in the professor's comments about their own writing, they learn what they have done well and what needs to be changed and improved.

Writing effective critiques, though, is not an easy task. Virtually every legal writing professor--whether a novice or a seasoned veteran--finds that he or she has to work hard to write critiques that teach as well as evaluate. Here are a few tips that will make the task at bit easier and, based on our experience, make the critiques more effective with your students.

1.    *Limit the number of comments you write on any given paper.*

Over-commenting, particularly on weak papers, tends to overwhelm and frustrate students. Rather than strive for comprehensive commenting, strive to write no more on a student's paper than he or she can be reasonably expected to assimilate. To avoid commenting on every little thing, determine what your priorities are before critiquing a stack of papers (see next tip) and stay focused on those priorities. Be sure to let your students know that you are being selective about your comments, though, so that they don't assume that everything left unmarked is perfect.

If you are hand writing comments, you may also want to use pencil (so that you can change your mind about what you say if you need to) or any color of ink besides red. Many students complain that red ink comments make their papers appear to "bleed." If you are typing your comments, consider using the "reviewing" function on your computer.  In Word, for example, you can access the reviewing function toolbar under the "View" pull-down list.   Select "toolbars" and then "reviewing."  The reviewing function will allow you to insert comments in bubbles next to the student's writing and make recommendations about how the students can edit their writing.

2.    *Develop teaching and critiquing priorities.*

Know what you want to teach, design assignments around those priorities, and then critique student writing with those priorities in mind. Develop a checklist that can be used when writing comments to ensure that you stay focused on your teaching priorities. Remember to consider big issues like content and organization before small issues like word choice and punctuation.

3.   *Give positive feedback as well as negative criticism.*

Students need to know what they have done well along with what they have done poorly. Positive comments that identify strengths in the writing help students know what they can build on or repeat in other writing projects. Positive comments also provide some encouragement and make it easier to accept suggestions about what needs to be changed. So that the students get more than just general encouragement from the positive comments, try to say how or why something they have done is good rather than just a "good" in the margins.

4.   *Write holistic end comments as well as margin comments.*

"End comments," whether they are written at the end of a paper or attached as a cover sheet to the paper, give an overview critique of the paper. Use end comments to synthesize the various points you make in the margin comments and to develop some priorities for the next time the student writes.

Although there is no specific format for end comments, many seasoned legal writing professors report that they typically begin an end comment on a positive note by discussing the strengths of the paper and then move to a discussion of its weaknesses. The weaknesses are often presented as a numbered list so that the student can use it as a checklist when revising the current paper or when composing the next paper. Many legal writing professors try to limit the list to 2-4 weaknesses so that they don't overwhelm the student. Some tie the margin and end comments together with a numbering system.

5.   *When possible, tie the comments to the text, class, and conferences.*

Comments on the students' papers are the principal way legal writing faculty have of working with a student to show him or her how what was taught in the text, class, or a conference should be applied in his or her writing. There are numerous ways in which your comments can make the connections between the student's own writing and the other components of the course. For example, for points about grammar and punctuation, you may want to send students directly to specific pages in the text. When you see a student making an effort to apply what you have discussed in class, your margin or end comments can show the connection between the student's work and a lecture or class discussion. You may also want to tell a student to do some specific revising before coming in for a conference.

6.   *Adopt a professional tone.*

When pointing out weaknesses in the writing, be sure to use a professional and encouraging tone. Resist the temptation to let your own anger, frustration, or even exasperation show, even if the paper in front of you is the tenth to make the same mistake. As a general rule, do not write comments that suggest that you believe a student did not work hard on the writing. Through your tone, make it clear that you are critiquing the paper, not the student.

7.     *Avoid ambiguous comments or marks.*

Students rarely find one-word comments like "vague" or "awk" useful. Circling or underlining without more explanation puts the student in the position of guessing what you were thinking. A question mark in the margin is equally frustrating for most students. As much as is humanly possible, write comments that are specific enough to be easily understood.

8.     *Write legibly or type your comments.*

9.     *Think through how you are going to survive the critiquing process.*

Many legal writing professors say that critiquing and grading are the most difficult parts of their job. You may be able to relieve some of the pressure of critiquing, however, by designing your courses so that you stagger some of the assignment due dates so that everything that needs to be read and commented on does not come in at one time. Seasoned legal writing faculty differ widely about how they approach a stack of papers (some recommend pacing yourself and doing a few papers every day; others recommend carving out a block of time and devoting it just to critiquing papers), but all are quite vocal about not procrastinating and making sure the papers are returned to students within a reasonable timeframe so that the writing is still fresh enough in the students' minds for the comments to be relevant to them.

10.    *Continue to learn as much as you can about critiquing.*

Because critiquing student papers is such a significant part of the legal writing professor's job, it is important not to become complacent about it once you have developed a reasonably successful approach. Talk to legal writing colleagues, read sample critiques from experienced legal writing faculty, read about commenting and grading in the professional literature, and stay tuned in to what your students say about your critiques of their papers.

---

1 *See* Anne M. Enquist, *Critiquing Law Students' Writing: What the Students Say Is Effective,* 2 *Legal Writing* 145 (1996); Hunter M. Breland and Frederick M. Hart, *Defining Legal Writing: An Empirical Analysis of the Legal Memorandum,* LSAC Research Report Series (1994); and Anne M. Enquist, *Critiquing and Evaluating Law Students' Writing: Advice from 35 Experts,* 22 Seattle U. L. Rev.1119 (1999).

## *Diagnosing Student Writing Problems*

**BEYOND LABELLING STUDENT WRITING PROBLEMS:**
**WHY WOULD A BRIGHT PERSON MAKE THIS MISTAKE?**
(reprinted from the September 1989 issue of The *Second Draft,* the bulletin for the Legal Writing Institute)

Most of us would be annoyed, perhaps enraged, if we went to a doctor about a problem and he or she merely labelled our malaise and left it at that. A diagnosis such as "Yes, Mr. Smith, you do have a skin rash" is almost as useless as the more specific "you have eczema, "unless it is followed by an explanation of what may have caused the problem and certainly what will cure it.

The relationship between patients and doctors is not all that different from that of law students and their legal writing professors. Unfortunately, though, our comments on their papers can often seem like mere labelling of writing problems with little direction toward "cure" and even less toward understanding what caused the problem in the first place. For example, a student who is told his paper "needs to be better organized" probably hasn't learned anything new. He knew it was a mess. What he wants and needs are 1) an explanation of why he isn't organizing the material well and 2) some organizing strategies that will solve the problem.

More and more legal writing professors seem to be willing and able to help students with that second need. They offer students suggestions on how their writing problems can be solved, so the "rash is cured" --for now. For this one paper, the student knows what he could have done to organize it better.

But what about the first need? The need to know why the problem occurred in the first place. Precious few legal writing professors seem to be willing to tackle this can of worms. And perhaps for good reasons. Unlike the medical profession, we have not developed our "science" (art?) to the point where there are generally accepted reasons for most student writing problems. We are left to second guessing, following hunches, and other revolutionary behavior for teachers such as asking students how they think and write. What's more, getting to the root of the problem is time-consuming. Very time-consuming. At the very least it requires more thought at the point the professor recognizes and labels the problem and more written comments as the professor explains what he or she guesses is the source of the problem. Quite often it will require a conference with the student.

Oh no, the groans begin. That will be impossible. It already takes me X number of days to wade through a stack of papers. What you are suggesting sounds like even more work. Perhaps. But what is the alternative? If we don't try to get at the source of the problem, most of our effort will be wasted anyway. If we are going to work this hard, why not make it count for something in the long run?

What I am proposing then, is that legal writing professors adopt a "best guess/talk-to-the-student" approach to uncovering the cause of individual students' writing problems.

Some examples might help to illustrate how this approach may work. The following cover letter for a resume was written by a law student who, from her participation in class, seemed to be bright and capable of handling law school work. She wanted the job she was applying for, so one can assume that she was sufficiently motivated to do her best on the letter.

**EXAMPLE A**

Dear Ms. Thompson:

Presently I am a first year student at the University of Puget Sound School of Law. Although I have only one grade on file, my G.P.A. is 3.35. I have recieved work-study funding during the 1984-85 academic year, and I expect my eligibility to continue through the 1985-86 academic year.

Prior to coming to Law School, I dealt with the public continuously in several positions as well as acting as a liason between my employer and their clients. Invaluable experience was also gained working with others as a team and trying to accomplish a common goal.

The Attorney General's Office provides a unique opportunity for learning which few employers can provide. Your Education and Human Rights Divisions intrest me most, although I would be willing to work in any one of your Divisions.

I am applying for a summer clerk position, my understanding being that the position will continue through the 1985-86 academic year. Throughout my first year at Law School, I have worked part-time and have been able to organize my time well enough to achieve optimum results in both school and work. I am certain that employment with the Attorney General's Office would be mutually beneficial.

I look foward to meeting your representative in February.

Sincerely,

Student X * * * *

A superficial diagnosis of this student's writing problems would include comments about grammar, mechanics, spelling and cliches, just to mention a few. For simplicity's sake, let's focus on the spelling first. Historically, this is just the kind of writing problem that professors label, possibly even chastise students about, but leave at that.

But why does a bright student make such spelling errors? Several possibilities come to mind, but before jumping to any conclusions, we should examine the misspellings and see if there is any pattern in the errors.

recieved     liason     intrest     foward

Sometimes patterns don't emerge, but in this case all the spelling errors occur in the middle of words. Perhaps the student has a hearing loss that keeps her from differentiating sounds in unaccented syllables.

Another good guess about the cause of the misspellings is that the student simply "does not care." It is not uncommon for law students to have the attitude that correct spelling is not a goal worthy of their attention. If this proves to be the case, the professor should then work to find out why this attitude exists. We should assume that our students have good reasons for their attitudes, and that we can have little effect in changing an attitude unless we understand the underlying reasoning.

In this example, carelessness might be the "best guess" about why this student spells poorly. The other errors in capitalization and grammar also suggest carelessness and a lack of commitment to error-free writing, although lack of pronoun agreement (employer/their), the lack of parallelism (dealt/acting), and the usage error ("continuously" rather than "continually") may also come from a lack of grammatical knowledge.

When asked about these errors in a writing conference, this student said she has always had problems with "the basics" in her writing. Not surprisingly, she did not seem to be overly concerned about the errors until she realized how her reader, a potential employer, might react to them. It simply had not occurred to her that she might not get an interview because of them. Further discussion revealed that in fact she did not know how to spell "received," "liaison," and "interest," that "foward" was a proofreading error, that she capitalized words when "they were important, " that she understood parallelism and pronoun agreement, but that the distinction between" continually" and continuously" was new to her.

The most important insight the professor gained from the conference was that the student was a speed reader. Typically this woman would pick up a novel and finish it in one evening. And, while most of us would assume that speed reading would be a tremendous advantage, it became increasingly clear that it was directly responsible for many of her writing problems. This student was trying to "speed proofread," which is almost a contradiction in terms. Once she forced herself to slow down she saw "foward" and the lack of parallelism and pronoun agreement.

Speed reading was also connected to her misspelling. As a reader she rarely looked at the middle of words. Without that constant reinforcement that most of us get, she was left with a dim mental image of how the middles of words look. To compensate for this, her professor suggested a technique from Mina Shaughnessey's book <u>Errors and Expectations</u>,[1] writing out words she consistently misspells with the trouble area enlarged, i.e., <u>recEIved</u>.

What we still have not addressed, though, is probably the most serious deficiency in this student's writing: her tendency to use cliches and almost meaningless expressions. In the writing conference, the professor asked her about three specific phrases in the letter, "unique opportunity," "optimum results," and "mutually beneficial." When pressed,

---

[1] Mina P. Shaughnessy , <u>Errors and Expectations: A Guide for the Teacher of Basic Writing</u> (New York: Oxford U. Press, 1977), pp. 160-186.

the student admitted that they held little specific meaning for her and that she used them when she did not know exactly what she wanted to say.

Again, we have the picture of the speed reader --the person who skims the surface of a piece of writing, one who does not assume that every word might be meaningful. To change this attitude, the professor had to demonstrate to the student how readers react to vague abstractions. This was done by simply giving the student her cover letter along with three others that were well written and much more specific. After carefully reading them all, the student admitted that there was nothing memorable in her letter (other than the errors) and that she would not have hired herself or even given herself an interview. Her attitude about most writing being relatively insignificant began to change as soon as she saw what effect it might have on her future.

Identifying attitudes that are at the root of writing problems is akin to identifying false assumptions that result in writing problems. Both require the evaluator to assume that the writer has a good reason for doing what he or she is doing and that once that reason is identified and examined, the student may be able to make a break-through. Example B is an excerpt from a memorandum written by a student at the top of her law class.

## EXAMPLE B

I.      Subject Matter Jurisdiction

Washington requires personal jurisdiction over both parties and subject matter jurisdiction in child custody cases. In re Marriage of Hall, 25 Wash. App. 530, 533 (1980). A Washington court which is competent to decide child custody matters has subject matter jurisdiction to make an initial custody decree or to modify a custody decree if Washington was the child's home state within six months before the custody action begins, and if the child is not present in Washington because a person claiming custody or for other reasons removes and retains the child from the state, and if a parent or person acting as a parent continues to live in Washington. In re Marriage of Myers, 92 Wash. 2d 113, 117 (1979) (quoting U.C.C.J.A.).

Prior to the adoption of U.C.C.J.A., a court had jurisdiction in child custody actions if it had personal jurisdiction over the parties and subject matter jurisdiction. Hall, 25 Wash. App. at 533. Subject matter jurisdiction depended on the child's domicile which followed that of the parent with legal custody. Id. The technical subtleties of the domicile concept were irrelevant to the custody proceeding's paramount concern, the child's welfare. Myers, 92 Wash. 2d at 115 (citing In re Miller, 86 Wash. 2d 712, 721-22 (1976)). A major change in custody jurisdiction came when the court considered the Myers case where the father had fled the state with the children. Under the domicile rule, since both parents had legal custody, the children would take the domicile rule because it would place the fleeing parent in a strong tactical position and instead held that personal jurisdiction over both parents gives state court jurisdiction in custody actions. Id. The most recent change in the custody jurisdiction occurred in 1979 when Washington adopted the U. C. C.J .A. The Act provides for jurisdiction based on the child's home state when the action begins, or if a fleeing parent has taken the child out of the state and the other parent still lives in the state, on the child's home state within six months from the start of the custody action. Id. at II7.

\* \* \* \*

Here the student has grasped a complex legal concept and explained it accurately, but her presentation of the material is an obstacle to the reader's understanding. The reader has to wrestle with some unusually long sentences and paragraphs. Typically, a professor's margin comments would point out both problems and may even suggest to the student how and where to break some of the sentences and paragraphs. Again, this might remedy the problem for this one paper, but the real question that should be asked is why the student wrote the overly long sentences and paragraphs in the first place. In this case, the student was operating under two false assumptions --one she had fabricated herself, another passed along as wisdom from an earlier writing class.[2] Sentence #2 demonstrates the first false assumption: that an entire law or legal concept is " one idea" and therefore must fit into one sentence. (This false assumption is reinforced when students read the law, court opinions, or other legal writing.) The student knew 83 words was a mental overload, even for the most conscientious of readers, but she thought she had no other options.

Similarly, she knew the second paragraph was too long, but she had been taught that each paragraph fully developed one key point, --here, the court's jurisdiction. She had not heard of paragraph blocks,[3] and furthermore, breaking the paragraph into three shorter paragraphs (before sentences #6 and #9) would leave her with a two-sentence paragraph, something else she thought she could not do.

Contributing to the problem of the overly long sentences were some avoidance tactics common among student writers. Students who don't know how to use colons or tabulation, for example, are often forced into packing a long list inside an already lengthy sentence. Others will try to avoid using semicolons out of some "semicolon mystique" or out of fear of making a mistake. Consequently, two ideas that could be neatly balanced or contrasted in main clauses separated by a semicolon are put

---

[2] It is always a good idea to ask a class what they were taught they could not do in writing. Besides such commonplace myths as "Never begin a sentence with 'and' or any other conjunction" and "never write a one-sentence paragraph, " students may tell you that they thought they could not start a sentence with "because" or "however" or that every paragraph had to have 3-5 sentences, no more, no less. Whatever the myths, once they are exposed as myths, the students gain some freedom in their writing options.

[3] Lynn B. Squires and Marjorie Dick Rombauer, Legal Writing in a Nutshell (St. Paul, Minn.: West, 1982) pp. 35-36.

together in one overwhelming maze of compound subjects with endless modifiers and compound verbs.

Guessing that the student writer of Example B was avoiding these marks of punctuation did not require a sleuth. The entire memorandum, which was over ten pages did not contain a single colon or semicolon. Trying to write without these punctuation marks limited the student's writing repertoire and frequently forced her into less than effective sentence structures.

Not all student writing problems show up in clear-cut patterns like the misspellings in Example A or the avoidance of colons and semicolons in Example B. Professors trying to employ the "best guess" approach to uncovering the cause of student writing problems sometimes find themselves grasping at straws in an effort to come up with some reasonable explanation for why a bright person would make this mistake. At this point it is often best to rely on the second half of the approach -- "talk to the student." Occasionally they will know exactly why they did what they did, even if they don't recognize that it led to poor writing. More often, it takes both the student and professor to piece together the underlying reasoning. Whoever discovers the source of the problem, though, is unimportant. That it is discovered, and then addressed and cured" (and not just for one paper) is the kind of lasting change that this approach hopes to facilitate.

# *Conducting Individual Writing Conferences*

When it comes to teaching someone how to write, there is probably no better method than the one-on-one writing conference. Admittedly, writing conferences do have some drawbacks, most notably the amount of time and energy they take. But when they are done well, that time and energy can be an important investment in that student's progress.

It is not easy to conduct effective writing conferences. Like all teaching, writing conferences require a considerable amount of thought, planning, and on-your-feet expertise. Unfortunately, though, it is tempting for legal writing faculty to rely too much on their on-your-feet expertise and, because of lack of planning, lose some of the potential writing conferences have.

A.    Develop a Conference Policy

Before beginning to offer writing conferences for your students, do two things: develop a policy about writing conferences and inform your students about that policy. We recommend that your policy about conferences focus on two points:
- planning for the conference by both the student and the legal writing professor, and
- timing of the conferences.

1. Planning

The most productive writing conferences are ones for which both the student and the professor have prepared. To accomplish this, have students submit a copy of their paper (or part of their paper) to you ahead of time with specific questions and topics they want to discuss in the conference. Receiving the papers, questions, and topics in advance allows you to prepare for the conference. It also forces the students to reflect more about what they want to accomplish in the conference.

If you were the one to recommend the conference for a specific purpose, tell the student in advance what the focus of the conference will be. It is often a good idea to require the student to do some preparation for such a conference. For example, if the student is having problems with organization, have the student prepare an after-the-fact outline of the paper and bring it to the conference. For other types of writing problems, you may want to assign specific sections of *Just Writing*.

2. Timing

Developing a policy about the timing of conferences is critical for your own emotional well-being. Most legal writing professors find that writing conferences the day before a paper is due and ones immediately after a graded paper is returned are unproductive. Conferences the day before a paper is due can be productive if you limit them to" quick questions." Students who wish to come in to discuss the law or the overall organization of their paper, however, simply do not have time to benefit from such a conference so close to the deadline. Consequently, you will probably want to tell students to use conference times right before the paper for questions about sentence construction, grammar, and the like.

Conferences immediately after a graded paper is returned tend to be "venting" sessions. Students who are unhappy about the grade will want to come in and debate the merit of their writing, sometimes even before they have read and carefully considered the written comments you put on the paper. Declaring a moratorium on conferences for 24 or 48 hours after a set of papers has been returned allows for a cooling off period. In other words, unless you want to help students through their emotional reaction to certain grades, do not offer conference appointments until you think the students will be able to talk rationally about what they need to work on in their writing.

B. Set a Collaborative Tone

Perhaps the key to effective writing conferences is to keep the responsibility for the writing in the students' hands. For this reason, resist the urge to become your students' editor. The role we recommend is closer to that of a collaborative expert reader.

1.      Sit side-by-side and keep the pen in the student's hand.

Logistically, writing conferences are more collaborative if the student and the legal writing professor are both looking at the paper together. This may mean re-arranging office furniture so that you can sit side-by-side, as well as giving up the powerful behind-the-big-desk position in the room.

If you can, try to keep the pen or pencil making the changes to the paper in the student's hand, not your hand. This simple practice reinforces the idea that you are not going to "fix the paper for them" and that you are not going to co-opt their work. (Although an occasional conference in which a student watches you edit his or her paper may be profitable, by and large students need to be the ones making the changes.)

2.      Ask questions rather than make pronouncements.

Obviously, you can and should make suggestions to students about their writing, but it is the students who must ultimately decide whether to incorporate the suggestions into their work. Rather than make pronouncements about the writing, ask questions. Find out how the student is thinking through the issue before trying to impose your own approach. As an expert reader, you can certainly comment about what you found clear or confusing, what you found precise or ambiguous. You can then help your students try to solve their writing problems, but try not to solve the problems for them.

One effective technique for conferences is to respond to the writing, not as a teacher/evaluator, but rather as a person who intends to use the writing, the real world reader. This type of role-playing makes it easier for students to see if their writing "works."

3.     Praise what was done well.

It is easy to slip into the habit of commenting only on the problems in a student's writing. The unstated assumption in this approach is that students only need to hear about what they need to change.

Admittedly, false or faint praise is unhelpful. Genuine praise, on the other hand, is essential. Not only does it encourage the student and build confidence, it also helps the student develop judgment about writing. As novices, students have fewer ways (than do expert legal readers) of judging what works and what doesn't. Consequently, before revising, they need to know if they did something well, or they just may take it out of the final version.

C.     Decide What to Teach -- What Does This Student Most Need to Know Next?

One important reason for getting the student's paper before the conference is that you will want to decide what you think the student should work on next. This is particularly true when the student is having serious problems and seems to be unable to decide what topics or questions should be the focus of a conference. In such cases, it is all too easy to be distracted by surface errors in the writing and neglect the larger, more significant problems, unless you have been able to do some diagnostic work on the paper in advance.

1.     Address the big issues first.

When faced with seriously flawed writing, be sure to address the big issues first. First check the student's thought process: has he or she identified the correct issues, correctly interpreted the law, understood who the reader is and what the document's purpose is? Second, check the student's organization, both large-scale and small-scale. Third, look at sentence structure and other writing issues at the sentence level. Finally, look at mechanics and other small surface issues such as citation, punctuation, and spelling.

2.     Teach less but be thorough about what you do teach.

For some reason, most students tend to progress most rapidly when their legal writing professor is selective about his or her advice. Too much advice, even when it is all good advice, tends to overwhelm students and confuse them about priorities. On the average, then limit yourself to no more than three points in a conference, especially if one or more of the points concern a big issue in writing.

D.    Provide Closure at the End of the Conference

A good writing conference, like any good composition, needs closure. The best closure is for the student to summarize, in his or her own words, what the key points were in the conference and then project how to apply those points to his or her writing, either in a revision of the paper that was discussed or in the next assignment.

If it seems awkward to ask the student to do the summarizing, the legal writing professor can be the one to do it. Either way, it is critical that the conference does not just end, but that it concludes.

Experience has taught that conferences that drift to an end often lose their focus. For example, the legal writing professor may be tempted to add just one more minor point, only to leave the student with *that* point as his or her strongest impression. Even more common, the student may have understood the key points in the conference at the time of the conference only to find that that understanding has begun to evaporate by the time he or she needs to use those points. Summarizing the key points of the conference in their own words reinforces those points for the students. It also gives the legal writing professor a quick opportunity to doublecheck the students' understanding.

# *Collaborative Learning*

Small groups. Some students love them. Other students hate them. But whether they love them or hate them, all students need them.

Students need small groups for two reasons. They need them because collaborative learning is an effective technique for teaching students how to apply rules and conventions, and they need them because collaborative learning teaches the interpersonal skills that are so essential to today's practice of law. Thus, although some students may resist small group work because it forces them to assume the role of an active learner and to interact with their classmates, it is exactly these two features that make collaborative learning so valuable.

Collaborative learning is not, however, appropriate for all students, in all situations, at all times. Some groups of students are simply too resistant for collaborative learning to work well, and although students can (and do) acquire information through collaborative learning, collaborative learning is not the most efficient method for transmitting information.

In addition, collaborative learning should not be viewed as an easy way to fill a class hour. It requires as much preparation as the most carefully drafted lecture and as much forethought as the most artfully scripted class discussion. Students must be prepared, the exercise planned, and the logistics of dividing students into groups must be thought through.


A. Train your Students to Work in Small Groups

Some students have not had experience working in small groups. Thus, although they know what is expected of them in the traditional teacher-centered classroom, they may be at a loss when assigned to work on a project with their peers. Other students may have had experience working in small groups, but it was not a positive experience because the students were not trained in effective small group learning techniques.

Consequently, you will probably need to train your students to work in small groups. This can be done indirectly, by modeling the appropriate discussion skills during class discussion and group exercises, or directly, by providing your students with formal training in small group dynamics. Whichever method you use, make sure that your students know what it is that you are trying to accomplish and why you believe collaborative learning to be the most effective method of accomplishing that goal. In addition, make sure that you demonstrate, through your preparation of the exercises and your use of the products that the groups produce, that you value small group work.

B.    Provide Your Students with the Information that They Need to Complete the Task

Collaborative learning only works when the students have the information that they need to complete the task. They cannot draft an issue statement unless they know what function an issue statement serves, what information should be included in one, and what format is appropriate. Similarly, they cannot formulate arguments and counterarguments if they are not familiar with the law and the acceptable forms of arguments. Thus, before assigning a small group exercise, provide your students with the necessary background information, either through a reading assignment or lecture. In addition, model for your students the type of behavior you want them to engage in. For example, before asking groups to draft topic sentences, make sure that your students have read the applicable section in *Just Writing* and that as a class, you have either helped students draft model topic sentences or helped them critique a number of samples.

Also remember to sequence the exercises. Early in the course, exercises should be relatively straightforward. Don't ask students to do much more than practice what it is that you have demonstrated. Conversely, later in the course, make the exercises more demanding.

C.    Divide Students into Groups

Once you have divided students into groups, you have lost them. They focus on the other members of their groups and not on the instructions that you are trying to give. As a consequence, make it a practice to explain the task before you assign students to groups.

In general, groups of three to five work best. The number of students put in each group will vary, however, depending on the nature of the exercise. If you are asking the students to produce a written product, use smaller groups; if you want students to brainstorm, use slightly larger groups.

Three methods can be used to assign students to groups: students can be allowed to form their own groups, students can be assigned to groups randomly, or students can be assigned to groups based on predetermined criteria. In deciding which method to use, consider the composition of the class, the abilities and personalities of the students within the class, and what the groups are to accomplish. Also keep in mind that groups tend to work better when the students in the group know each other well enough to make communication possible without investing time in "breaking the ice" but when they are not "best friends." Also remember that more learning occurs when the members of the group have different backgrounds and perspectives.

You will also need to provide each group with an appropriate place to work. When the exercise requires the group to work for an extended period of time at a complex task, it is usually best to send each group to a conference room or empty classroom. For other exercises, have each group meet around tables or desks in a different corner of the classroom. Noise is not usually a problem: when there are three or more groups working in the same classroom, students are not usually distracted by individual voices, and the noise seems to induce productive conversation.

D.      Structure the Exercise

At least initially, structure the task carefully. Prepare written instructions that provide the group with step-by-step guidance, telling them what they should do and the approximate amount of time that they should spend on each task.

If all the members of the group do not know each other, the first instruction should require each member of the group to spend one or two minutes introducing himself or herself to the other members of the group. This is a relatively non-threatening activity, and it gives each member of the group an opportunity to speak.

Each group should then be instructed to select a "recorder." The students selected as the recorders should be told that they are not the chairperson; as recorder their job is to record the group discussion and product and to report to the rest of the class. If you use collaborative learning frequently, make sure that each student takes a turn playing the role of reporter.

After the group has selected a recorder, it is then ready to begin work on the task itself. The task should be divided into its component parts and the parts should be arranged sequentially. The instructions and questions should take the students, step-by- step, down a path that you envisioned when you designed the exercise.

As part of the exercise, each group should be required to produce something. For example, groups can be asked to prepare a list or outline or to draft or redraft an issue statement, statement of facts, or argumentative heading. By being forced to produce something, each group becomes accountable and is forced to move toward consensus, a process that makes students deal with the questions more critically than they might otherwise.

It is also best if the students have something at stake in doing the exercise. The most successful exercises are those in which students are doing something that is directly related to a graded assignment. For example, students may work with the group to prepare a first draft of the rule section for their memo or brief that the students can then use in their appellate briefs.

After the groups have completed the exercise, each group should report back to the class as a whole or share its product with the other groups. Two methods can be used. The best method is to reconvene the class and ask each reporter, in turn, to share the group's product or the results of its discussion. During these reports, play an active role: ask the reporters specific questions, and encourage the reporters to explain their group's decisionmaking process and to contrast their group's product with the products produced by the other groups. A less desirable but more efficient method is to have each group turn in their "product" and have the products photocopied and distributed to each member of the class.

E.    Decide on the Professor's Role in the Group

Deciding to use collaborative learning also means deciding to change the role you play in the classroom. When you use more traditional teaching methods, you are the center of attention. From a position in front of the classroom, you control both who speaks and, in large part, what is said. In contrast, when you use collaborative learning you relinquish, at least temporarily, center stage. Your role is now that of director and not the primary actor.

It will take time for both you and your students to become accustomed to your new role. You can, however, ease and speed up the transition by doing the following.

After dividing the students into groups, leave the classroom for ten to fifteen minutes. Go the faculty lounge and have a quick cup of coffee. Although walking out the door is difficult, and to some extent risky, you need to make it clear to your students that you are giving them control of their own learning.

When you return to the classroom, don't immediately join a group. While you pretend to be busy with some task, listen to what is going on in the groups. If, after listening to the groups, you determine that the groups are working in the way that you intended leave them alone; at least at first, collaborative learning works best when each group works through the exercise on its own.

If, however, you determine that a group is either not working on the task or is not working through the task in the way that was intended, join the group as a group member. Pull a chair into the circle or sit around the table with the group. Listen for a while and then, when the opportunity presents itself, join the discussion as a model group member. Suggest another way of thinking about the question, ask someone else in the group for his or her opinion, or respond to a statement made by another group member. When the group is back on track, quietly excuse yourself

Note:

If a student approaches you while you are listening to the groups, answer legitimate questions but resist the student's attempts to force you back into the more traditional role of "professor."

While the groups are working, you have one other responsibility. As director you need to monitor the progress of the groups. Periodically approach each group and inquire about how far they are in the exercise, and once or twice during the class hour announce how much time is left.

## A FINAL NOTE

Collaborative learning is not just an effective way of teaching; it is also a rewarding way to teach. Just as parents are proud of their children's growing independence, you too will be proud as you watch your students grow from students into members of the profession.

# Teaching Notes for the Chapters in *Just Writing*

Our assumption is that legal writing professors who are using this book are also using one or more other texts for their class, such as a research book, an analysis book, and a book on legal citation. For that reason, the Teaching Notes for many of the chapters begins with a "timing" suggestion for when to integrate the chapter into a legal writing course. The timing suggestion is generally followed by "suggested teaching methods."

You will also notice that we do not recommend that every chapter be assigned to every student. Most law students, for example, will not need the sentence grammar refresher that is in the beginning of Chapter 8; some, however, will. Other students who are struggling as writers may find the suggestions in Chapter 7 concerning eloquence are beyond their current ability; strong writers, on the other hand, will find it shows them what else they can do to improve. Obviously native speakers and writers of English will not need Chapter 10, which is written specifically for ESL law students. Our recommendation, then, is to use *Just Writing* flexibly—assigning some chapters for all students, but choosing specific chapters or sections to recommend to selected students.

**Chapter 1: Effective Writing: The Whole Paper**

**§ 1.1 The Psychology of Writing**

<u>Timing:</u>

Assign as reading at the same time that you assign the first memo assignment.

<u>Suggested Teaching Methods:</u>

Option 1: Have students create a schedule for the research and writing of the first memo.

Option 2: After students have completed their first or second research exercise, spend five or so minutes at the end of the class discussing with the class how each of them is organizing the research. Find out if students are using color coding, file folders, a tabbed notebook, computer files, or some other organizational method.

**§ 1.2 Outlines, Writing Plans, and Ordered Lists**

<u>General Comments:</u>

Each of the various strategies for creating an outline tends to appeal to a certain type of thinker/learner/writer. For example, people who are naturally collaborative and good talkers tend to benefit most from talking over their ideas with a colleague. People who have used different ways of organizing material as members of another profession may prefer to try an analogy or format they are more comfortable with (blueprints, flow charts). Holistic thinkers may find clustering appealing. Encourage students to use the strategy that feels most natural to them and to experiment with other strategies when whatever they are using isn't working.

<u>Suggested Teaching Methods:</u>

Option 1: On the day that you require students to bring an outline to class, spend five or so minutes discussing with them how each of them created the outline. Remind students that simple techniques such as "talk it over with a colleague" are used by countless successful lawyers. Tell them how you create outlines or organizational plans. Tell them about techniques you observed other lawyers using while in practice.

Option 2: As a class or in small groups, use one or more of the techniques to create an outline for whatever writing assignment the class is currently working on.

Option 3:    Occasionally a student who is having difficulty creating an outline will sign up for an individual writing conference.  In the conference, find out which, if any, of the strategies he or she has used, unsuccessfully for this project and successfully in the past for other writing projects.  Based on what the student tells you about his or her writing and thinking style, select, together, a strategy and work the student through the process using that strategy.   (The Three-Column chart is often effective when the student is feeling particularly overwhelmed by the material.)

## § 1.3  Drafting the Document

General Comments:

Creating a classroom atmosphere in which students are comfortable talking about their writing processes can help students view writing more positively.  For example, many legal writers have problems with procrastination.  Rather than pretend this problem does not exist, it is often valuable to spend some class time acknowledging the problem and then having students share how they overcome the tendency to procrastinate about writing.  Such discussions not only give students useful tips for dealing with writing problems, but they also go a long way toward creating a classroom community that is conducive to writing development.

There also appears to be some benefit to encouraging students to become more conscious of their own writing processes.

Suggested Teaching Method:

This section lists only a sampling of the many ways writers get themselves to write.  After assigning this section, ask your students how they "psyche themselves up" to do a writing assignment.  Consider asking them when and where they write best.  Under what conditions are they likely to write well: under what conditions are they likely to write poorly?

## § 1.4  Revising

Suggested Teaching Methods:

Option 1:    As a class, develop a revision checklist for the current writing assignment.

Option 2:    Students who sign up for individual writing conferences and who typically have problems organizing their writing can be required to do an after-the-fact outline of their draft before coming to the conference.  They should bring the outline and the draft with them to the conference, or they can be required to turn them in before the conference.

## § 1.5- § 1.7  Editing, Proofreading, Myths about Writing

<u>General Comments:</u>

If you are new at teaching legal writing, you may be amazed to find out how many myths there are about writing.  The dangerous thing about many of these myths is that students try to write by them.  They treat them as absolute rules, possibly because someone taught the myth to them as if it were a rule.

In Section 1.7, we tried to identify five of the more common myths that students apply as rules.  You will undoubtedly uncover more.  They will surface when you ask students why they did or didn't do something and they respond with something like "I thought you always had to . . ." or even more common "Well, I thought you never could . . . ."

<u>Suggested Teaching Methods:</u>

Option 1:    *early in the course*

Select a student sample of a draft that is of better than average quality.  If possible, the sample should contain typical problems such as imprecise language, wordiness, lack of transitions, and lack of topic sentences.  Using a document reader or transparency (students should have photocopies), demonstrate how you would edit it.  Be sure to show that editing is both a process of addition and subtraction.  Be sure to read the sample aloud to demonstrate how one can "hear" some writing problems.  Be sure to comment positively on the good features of the writing.  (See Appendix A "Using Student Samples in Class.")

Option 2:    *later in the course*

When the students learn more about editing, you can then break them into groups of two or three and ask them to edit two or three paragraphs from a student sample that is of better than average quality.  Have some of the groups show their edits to the class, either on a document reader or transparency, and discuss the choices they made.

Option 3:    *proofreading*

"Doctor" a section from a sample memo by adding a few errors that should be caught in proofreading.  One or two of the errors should be substantively significant (wrong date, wrong dollar amount), several errors should be typical typos (missing small word, transposed letters), and at least one name should be wrong.  More of the errors should occur later in the section.  Make a game out of who can find all the errors.  Ask those who are successful at finding the errors what proofreading method they used.

Option 4:     *proofreading*

On the day before a writing assignment is due, allow students to pair up to proofread each other's memo.

**Chapter 2: Connections Between Paragraphs**

**§ 2.1 Headings**

General Comments:

Some legal writing professors have strong preferences about whether students should use headings in legal writing. Be sure to let your students know what your preferences are.

Be sure to point out to students that Option 3 in the examples of substitute headings is a good heading for a memo, not a brief.

**§ 2.2 Roadmaps and Signposts**

Suggested Teaching Methods:

Option 1: *roadmaps*

Select two or possibly three different sample roadmap paragraphs from student drafts. One sample should be a relatively unsophisticated roadmap paragraph, and at least one other sample should be a better roadmap. Have the students read the samples and then ask them which roadmap is helpful to the reader and why.

Option 2: *roadmaps and signposts*

Ask students to highlight roadmap paragraphs and signposts in their own drafts before handing them in.

Option 3: *roadmaps and signposts*

To demonstrate the importance of roadmaps and signposts, give the students a copy of a well-written memo or brief from a case with which they are not familiar, but delete the roadmap paragraph and all signposts. Students will invariably find this version confusing and difficult to read. After the students have read this version, show them the version with the roadmap and signposts.

## Chapter 3: Effective Paragraphs

### § 3.1-§ 3.3 The Function of a Paragraph, Paragraph Patterns, Unity and Coherence in Paragraphs

<u>General Comments:</u>

Although a student writer needs to know everything about writing before writing the first memo, it is not practical to try to each everything at once. When we make the mistake of trying to teach too much all at once, students inevitably learn less, not more. For this reason, we recommend that you focus on large-scale organizational issues (the basic format) first and then move to small-scale organization (the paragraph) second.

The purpose of these classes on paragraph writing is to emphasize to students that paragraph writing is not a random, catch-as-catch-can activity. Instead, paragraph writing is a deliberate, reflective act, perhaps even the primary way that writers exercise control over their material.

<u>Suggested Teaching Method:</u>

*Note: The following methods are more effective if the students have already read sections 4.3 and 8.7 on dovetailing and parallelism.*

Select and photocopy sample paragraphs from the students' first drafts, ideally one that lacks unity because the writer has added in a stray thought, one that lacks unity because the writer wasn't sure what point he or she was making in the paragraph, and one that has unity. Begin by showing the students the paragraphs that lack unity.

To determine if a paragraph has unity, ask students what the topic of the paragraph is. It often works well to phrase the question as "what point is the writer trying to make in this paragraph?" If the students have difficulty deciding or agreeing on the paragraph's point, then it obviously lacks unity. Point out that this kind of "grab-bag" paragraph is common in first draft writing as a writer gropes for the point he or she wants to make. Writers can revise for this problem by asking themselves "what's my point?" and then writing a topic sentence that helps them keep the paragraph under control.

The students may also find that all but part of the paragraph is unified around one point. In such cases, ask students what the writer should do with the part that seems to be out of place. Point out that associational thinking sometimes leads to stray sentences or that they may appear because the writer knows that the "stray point" needs to be discussed somewhere but he or she is unsure where to put it.

End by showing the students the paragraph that is unified and discussing what makes it unified.

For the same class, photocopy one or two sample paragraphs that demonstrate good coherence.  Have the student determine what are the key terms in one of the sample paragraphs and then go through that paragraph marking each time the term or a version of the term is used.  In the same paragraph or in the second sample paragraph, have the students mark the other coherence devices:  dovetailing, parallelism, and pronouns.

## § 3.4 - § 3.6  Paragraph Length, Topic and Concluding Sentences, Paragraph Blocks

Timing:

Assign these sections when the students are drafting or revising a memo.

General Comments:

Most law students have not been introduced to the concept of paragraph blocks, even though it is a critical feature of this type of writing.  For this reason, you may want to make it a point to emphasize paragraph blocks in class and to show students examples of how legal writers use them to organize complicated discussions.

Topic sentences, on the other hand, are old news to law students.  Nevertheless, many law students need to be reminded about the importance of topic sentences in expository prose.  Most law student who use topic sentences, though, use the unsophisticated variety discussed in § 3.5.1 that merely name the topic.  One way to move students toward writing better topic sentences (and consequently toward more sophisticated analysis) is to tell them to ask themselves "why am I using this case?" and then to incorporate their answer to that question into a topic sentence that introduces the case.  Another similar approach is to ask student what principle they are using the case(s) to illustrate and then have them set out that principle in the topic sentence.

Suggested Teaching Methods:

Option 1    After the students have read these sections, have them go back to the first memo they wrote and (1) examine the number of sentences in each paragraph, (2) determine if they used topic and concluding sentences for each paragraph, (3) select the paragraph that they think has the strongest topic sentence, (4) identify any paragraph blocks, and (5) determine if they are introduced by topic paragraphs.

Option 2    Working in pairs, have the students go through a section of each of their drafts of a memo, examining the length of each paragraph but focusing on whether the writer is using topic and concluding sentences.  If they agree that a paragraph would be improved by the addition of topic or concluding sentences, they should add them.  The students should then determine whether paragraph blocks are being used in the drafts and, if so, if they are introduced and concluded by topic and concluding paragraphs.

Option 3      Using photocopies or transparencies or both, go through a good quality draft of a memo as a class, looking at (1) paragraph length, (2) topic and concluding sentences, (3) paragraph blocks, and (4) topic and concluding paragraphs.

**Chapter 4: Connection Between Sentences**

**§ 4.1-§ 4.3 Generic Transitions, Orienting Transitions, Substantive Transitions**

<u>General Comments:</u>

Most students will be quite familiar with generic and orienting transitions, Substantive transitions, on the other hand, will be new for most students. Consequently, they may require more in-class teaching.

One common mistake students make is to edit out all transitions in an effort to be more concise. You will undoubtedly want to talk with them about finding the right balance between conciseness and a fluid writing style.

Notice that the five options listed below teach different points. For that reason, you will probably want to use more than one of them.

<u>Suggested Teaching Methods:</u>

Option 1     *focus on generic transitions*
Remove all the generic transitions from a section of a well-written sample memo. Have the students read this version, and ask if they consider it well written. Make sure that they see that it is not missing any content. Then show them the version with the generic transitions to demonstrate how the transitions are subtle guides through the material.

Option 2     *focus on generic and orienting transitions*
Using a well-written sample of a draft of a memo, have the students find and mark all the generic and orienting transitions. Then have the students find and mark all the generic and orienting transitions in their own draft.

Option 3     *focus on lack of transitions and incorrect transitions*
Alter a well-written sample of a student memo by deleting many of the transitions or replacing a transition with another inappropriate transition from a different category. Working as a class, determine where transitions need to be added or changed.

Option 4     *focus on substantive transitions*
Alter a well-written sample of a student-written memo by deleting all substantive transitions. Review with students what substantive transitions are, and have the students read this version and then show them the version containing the substantive transitions.

Option 5     *focus on substantive transitions*
Review with students what substantive transitions are and how they are formed. Then, using samples sections of drafts from their current memos (students'

names removed) in which students have made a "mental leap," have the students write substantive transitions that will carry the reader from the first point to the second. This can be done in pairs or with the entire class.

**Chapter 5: Effective Sentences**

<u>General Comments:</u>

The points made in Chapters 5 and 6 need to be emphasized throughout the course. Whether the students are writing memoranda, opinion letters, or briefs, they will need to apply the principles of good sentence writing and appropriate word choice. Consequently, it is best to assign these chapters early in the course and then return to the ideas in them throughout the course.

**§ 5.1 Active and Passive Voice**

<u>General Comments:</u>

Occasionally students confuse passive voice with past tense. This confusion is easily corrected by pointing out that passive voice concerns the relationship between the subject and the verb and past tense concerns the timeframe of the verb.

Some students have been taught or given the blanket advice to avoid the passive voice without also being given the explanation of why the active voice is *generally* preferable and when the passive voice is more effective than active voice. For this reason, emphasize that voice is a stylistic choice, not a grammar rule, and that writers need to understand the way voice works so that they can make informed choices about its use.

Some students have a strong tendency to overuse the passive voice. Such students benefit from an individual conference that focuses on this problem. Frequently, these students come to law school from professions or undergraduate majors in which passive voice writing is expected or even required. Lab reports from the natural sciences, for example, are usually written in passive voice.

<u>Suggested Teaching Method:</u>

Take a few minutes to review the difference between active and passive voice using a simple pair of sentences such as *The defendant drove the car home* and *The car was driven home by the defendant.* Point out that in the first sentence (which uses active voice) the subject, *the defendant*, is doing the verb, *drove*, and in the second sentence (which uses passive voice) the subject, *the car*, is having the verb, *was driven*, done to it.

Use the following chart to help students remember the difference between the two:

Active voice…subject is active
Passive voice…subject is passive

Discuss situations in which the active voice sentence would be the better choice and situations in which the passive voice would be the better choice.

Examples:
Active voice preferred when
    -the focus is on the defendant and his or her actions

    Passive voice preferred when
    -the focus in on the car

If the defendant admits that the car ended up at home but denies that he or she was the one who drove the car home, the passive construction *the car was driven home* is probably the best choice. Then, when relevant, point out choices writers make in using active and passive voice in sample papers discussed in class.

## § 5.2 Concrete Subjects

General Comments:

Students may also want to read Joseph Williams's extensive discussion of nominalizations in his book, *Style: Ten Lessons in Clarity and Grace*, 4th edition HarperCollins College Publishers, 1994.

Suggested Teaching Method:

As was the case with active and passive voice, these points can best be taught in context using samples of the students' writing. Although you will want to remind the students that not every sentence in legal writing can have a concrete subject, they should avoid the "nobody's home" style of writing that needlessly uses an abstraction as the subject of every sentence and needlessly nominalizes every verb.

Similarly, using samples of student writing, show students that most of the "it is _____ that" sentence openers can be edited out leaving an improved sentence, but remind students that this is general advice and not a blanket rule. Occasional use of such sentence openers can be effective. The point is that most legal writers overuse them to the detriment of their writing.

Example:

~~It is important to remember that~~ the McKibbins never signed a contract.

## § 5.3 Action Verbs

General Comments:

Most authorities on writing style agree that the place to begin working on a writer's style is with the verbs. If the writer chooses the right verb for the sentence, most of the other pieces begin to fall into place. For this reason, you may find it helpful to focus on the verbs first whenever you sense there is a problem with a student's writing style and you are having difficulty figuring out exactly what the problem is.

Suggested Teaching Method:

These points can best be taught in context using samples of the students' writing. In addition, one or two good examples of a series of revisions (see below) can demonstrate how a writer might edit out a weak sentence opener with a "to be" main verb, such as *there is,* end up with a passive voice construction that can then be revised to active voice.

The following example is based on a pair in the text.

Example:

*Original:*
There are four elements that must be proved to recover damages under the family car or purpose doctrine.

*First Revision:*
Four elements must be proved to recover damages under the family car or purpose doctrine.

*Second Revision:*
The plaintiff must prove four elements to recover damages under the family car or purpose doctrine.
Finally, if the students have read Section 4.3.1, you can add in a point about dovetailing.

*Third Revision:*
To recover damages under the family car or purpose doctrine, the plaintiff must prove four elements:  (list elements)

*Original:*
There are several factors that the court will rely on in deciding that the goods are specially manufactured.

*First Revision:*
The court will rely on several factors in deciding that the goods are specially manufactured.

*Second Revision:*
In deciding that the goods are specially manufactured, the court will rely on several factors:  (list factors)

You may want to develop an example and a series of revisions based on material the students will use in their current memo problem.

## § 5.4  Distance Between Subjects and Verbs

Suggested Teaching Method:

Have students select approximately two pages of the draft they are writing and mark the subjects and verbs of their sentences.  Besides looking at whether they are using active or passive voice (and why) and whether they have concrete subjects and action verbs, have them look at how many words separate each subject from its verb.

## § 5.5  Sentence Length

General Comments:

Students who write overly long sentences sometimes do so because they are trying to make simple ideas look complex or because they are novices using too many qualifiers in an effort to protect themselves.  It takes confidence to state a simple idea simply; it takes confidence to make a point boldly, without needless qualifiers.  As teachers of legal writing, then, our job is to help students develop judgment about what to do when.  Undoubtedly the best way to teach judgment about sentence length, indeed about all legal writing, is to constantly remind students to use their readers and the context in which the writing occurs as a basis for all writing decisions.

Suggested Teaching Method:

Have the students count the number of words in each sentence in their own drafts of a memo.  Have each determine his or her average sentence length.  Also ask students to look at whether there is some variety in their sentence length.  Remind them that readers can comprehend a fairly long sentence better if it is preceded or followed by shorter sentences.  Finally, have students look at their longest sentences and mark the units of meaning within the sentence.  Have them determine the length of each unit of meaning.

Example of marking units of meaning (marked by /):

The court found that the duties of a parole board member are functionally equivalent to that of a judge in at least two ways:/ (1) both render impartial decisions in cases and controversies that excite strong feelings  because the litigant's liberty is at stake,/ and (2) both face the same risk of constant unfounded suits by those disappointed by the decisions.

Sentence Total= 59 words
Units of Meaning=24/19/16 words respectively

Remind students that overall sentence length is not the only measure of readability. They must also look at the units of meaning within sentences because their readers will be processing the information on this basis, as well as on sentence length.

Also remind students that by reading their writing aloud, they will "hear" when a sentence is too long.

## § 5.6 Emphasis

<u>Timing:</u>

This section can be assigned when the students are revising a draft of a memo, but it works especially well when students are drafting briefs. You may also want students to review § 9.3 and § 9.5 on colons and dashes.

<u>Suggested Teaching Methods:</u>

Option 1    *emphasis in general*

Ask the students to list those facts that are most favorable to their client. From this list, have them select the one or two facts that are particularly favorable for their client or damaging to their opponent. Using the drafts of the statement of facts from their briefs, select 2 or 3 versions of how one of these particularly favorable facts was written up. (This can be done using transparencies, photocopies, or a document reader.) Have the class decide which of the versions succeed in emphasizing this fact effectively and how the writer achieved effective emphasis. Was one or more of the strategies in the section used? Were strategies other than those mentioned in the text used?

If time permits, have the students consider how they wrote about the second key fact they want to emphasize. If they are satisfied with their version, have them write it on a transparency or show their version with a document reader. If they are dissatisfied, give them a few minutes to revise it. Using the transparencies or document reader, repeat the earlier procedure of examining several versions and discussing what strategies each used to create emphasis.

Have students list those facts that are most unfavorable to their client. Remind them that although they must concede these points, they do not want to emphasize them. Further, given what they know about how to emphasize favorable facts, ask how they can de-emphasize unfavorable facts.

Based on their reading of Chapter 5, they should come up with most of the following strategies:

(1) Bury it in the middle of a sentence, in the middle of a paragraph, and if possible in the middle of a section;

(2) Include it in a long sentence and even a long paragraph, ideally surrounded by favorable facts;

(3) Admit it once and only once and spend a minimum of airtime stating the fact;

(4) State it in neutral, bland language.

Option 2     *emphasis in general*

Use a similar approach as option 1 but select favorable points for the client that should be made in the argument section.

Option 3     *single word emphasizers*

Discuss with students whether they agree with the text when it says that *clearly* is overused in legal language.  Ask whether they feel more persuaded by speakers or writers who use *clearly* for emphasis.  Using their drafts of the brief, have them search for uses of *clearly* and any other word that emerged in the discussion as being similarly misused.  (*Obviously* and *very* are other possibilities mentioned in the text.)

At this point, students may suggest that a word or phrase that is a key term in the memo they are writing is overused.  This is an ideal opportunity to discuss the difference between losing emphasis by thoughtlessly adding in weak modifiers and gaining emphasis by the deliberate repetition of key terms.

Option 4     *changing the normal word order*

Ask students to collect examples of sentences in which the normal word order is changed for emphasis.  Perhaps the most common well-known example is John Kennedy's "Ask not what your country can do for you; ask what you can do for your country."  Discuss why the "equivalent" sentence "don't ask what your country can do for you; ask what you can do for your country" lacks emphasis and is therefore less memorable.

Option 5     *repeating key words*

Ask students to identify their theory of the case, or their theme(s), and the key words that make up this theory, or theme.  Then have them go through the draft of their argument section and circle these key words and their variations.

Photocopy three different argument sections—one that does not weave in the key terms of the theme (often by using synonyms or forgetting to make explicit connections to the theme), one that overuses the key words, and one that finds the right balance.  Discuss all three.

**Chapter 6: Effective Words**

**§ 6.1 Diction and Precision**

<u>General Comments:</u>

Like the material in Chapter 5, the material in Chapter 6 needs to be emphasized throughout the course. Consequently, it is best to assign this chapter as early as possible in the course and then return to the ideas in it throughout the course.

<u>Suggested Teaching Methods:</u>

Discuss with students how learning the language of law is a little like learning a new dialect of one's own language. It is not an entirely different language, as German is different from Japanese, but it is a distinct variation, as the English spoken in the South is both different from and similar to the English spoken in Great Britain. Consequently, there are not just new words to learn, there are also new combinations of words (see "Typical Subject-Verb-Object Combinations" exhibit on page 107), new expectations, and new conventions.

Before they come to class, have students circle one or two word choices in their own drafts that caused them difficulty. Select three examples and photocopy enough of the surrounding language so that the class gets a sense of what the writer is trying to say.

For each word, first discuss the denotation, or dictionary definition. If the denotation suits the writer's purposes, then discuss the word's connotations. Make sure that enough members of the class share their connotations, or associations, with the word so that the writer has a sense of the word's flavor for different people. If the connotations of the original word do not work for the writer's purposes, have the class suggest other word choices.

This same exercise can be repeated for later memos, and it should definitely be repeated for the brief. When it is used for briefs, begin by asking the writer what he or she is trying to accomplish and what theme, or theory of the case, he or she wants to put forth. With this information as a backdrop, the class can discuss whether the selected word's denotation and connotation work.

Successful undergraduate writers, particularly English majors, may have some difficulty adjusting to the "same term for the same idea" axiom in legal writing. They have had years of being rewarded for showing off their vocabulary, so expect some grumbling and frustration as they learn to adapt to the expectations of legal writing.

## § 6.2 Conciseness

<u>Timing:</u>

After reading drafts of the first memo, you will want to refer some students to this section immediately. Assign the section to the entire class when the students are revising a memo or brief.

<u>General Comments:</u>

What is challenging about trying to teach conciseness is that in any typical legal writing class you will have students who are incredibly verbose and others who are terse and conclusory. Furthermore, students beginning a career in law have a difficult time determining when to cut an idea and when to expand upon one.

Conciseness, then, needs to be taught from at least two perspectives: conciseness in content and conciseness in expression. By conciseness in content, we mean knowing which ideas to put in and which ones to take out. By conciseness in expression, we mean making what points you need to make in few words.

<u>Suggested Teaching Method:</u>

Option 1 *conciseness of content*

Remind students that their touchstone for determining whether to include a point is always "does my reader need to know this?" The most common problem students have in this area is confusing what they as students and novice writers needed to know and what the reader, who is probably an attorney or judge, needs to know.

Issues that should come up in this discussion include the following:

- What do practicing attorneys or judges know based on education and experience?
- Does the reader need to know this piece of information before he or she can make the next decision?
- When does more information become overkill for this reader?
- How long of a document does this reader expect to get, and what happens if the writer frustrates these expectations, even for a good reason?
- (for memo writing) In giving you this assignment, did the reader want you to address this point?
- (for brief writing) If this point is omitted from the brief, does the client have a claim for ineffective assistance of counsel?

Option 2      *paring down quotations*

If the first writing assignment your class has requires analyzing a statute, make a transparency or copy of the entire statute. Students should have their own photocopies. As a group, discuss what part or parts of the statute are relevant. Using an overhead or document reader, discuss how to pare the statute down to the essentials. You may then want to break the class into pairs and ask each pair to write an effective lead-in to the quoted statute (see pages 241-242). This is also a good time to discuss how to use ellipses and brackets (pages 245-249) with quotations.

Option 3      *conciseness in general*

Select a sample draft that needs editing for conciseness. You may want to add more examples of wordiness to the sample draft. Using a transparency, document reader, or photocopies, discuss how to edit the sample draft. Yet another option is to break the class into groups and have each group come up with its own edit of the draft.

Option 4      *conciseness in general*

Have each student bring a copy of his or her draft of the current writing assignment to class. Working in pairs, have the students edit these drafts for conciseness. This option works best if the students' drafts are close to their final form

Remind students that the conventions of memo and brief writing are different from the conventions of exam taking. In exams, students must take their reader down the blind alley they explored, or they will be faulted for conclusory reasoning.

## § 6.3  Plain English v. Legalese

Timing:

Assign this section when the students are drafting or revising their briefs or when they are writing opinion letters. You may also want to assign § 6.4 and § 6.5 at the same time.

General Comments:

In the 16th edition of the *Bluebook*, Rule 7B on which foreign phrases to capitalize is clarified by several examples.

Russ VerSteeg's book *Essential Latin for Lawyers* (Carolina Academic Press, 1990) is a helpful resource for Latin phrases used in law.

Option 1    Point out examples of legalese whenever they appear in student examples used in class. For each instance, discuss whether the legalese was effective.

Option 2    Invite a judge or justice to speak to the class about legalese. Ask him or her to respond to specific examples of legalese, ideally ones that might appear in briefs for the case the students are working on.

Option 3    Bring in some form books so that students can see what they are, and photocopy one or two examples. Discuss the advantages and disadvantages of the boilerplate language in the examples.

Option 4    Discuss with the class whether there are any terms of art in the problem they are doing. If there is a disagreement about whether a given word or phrase is a true term of art, have the students apply the definition from Mellinkoff: Is the term specific and precise within this specialty?

Option 5    Show students examples of "shop talk" from other fields. Discuss when such shoptalk is appropriate and why it is useful in those situations (reasons should include such things as efficient communication, community bonding among professionals). Discuss when such shoptalk is inappropriate and why.

## § 6.4 Gender-Neutral Language

<u>Timing:</u>

If one of the memo problems or opinion letter assignments raises the issue of gender-neutral language, assign this section at that time. If not, assign with section 6.3 and 6.5 when students are drafting or revising their briefs.

<u>General Comments:</u>

Many students, both male and female, do not consider gender-neutral language to be a serious issue. For this reason, you may want to bring in respected members of the legal community to talk with them about it. Ardent feminists, on the other hand, may want to highlight their use of gender-neutral language to the point that the primary purpose of the document seems to have become an expression of the writer's politics. Remind students that unless that is their purpose, they should use gender-neutral language in a way that does not distract the reader from the document's true primary purpose. For example, they should use combinations like *himself or herself* sparingly, and certainly avoid using more than one such combination per sentence.

To make this issue immediately relevant to your class, consider writing into one of your memo or brief assignments an aspect that will naturally raise this issue. For example, if the law in your jurisdiction defines a landowner using *he*, make the client landowner female.

Suggested Teaching Methods:

Option 1    Whenever relevant, point out gendered (and gender-neutral) language in samples of student writing used in class. Also point out gendered and gender-neutral language in cases the students are reading. Ask the students what effect, if any, they think the language will have on a reader.

Option 2    Ask several female members of the class to react to hypothetical correspondence from their attorney that addresses them as the equivalent of *Mrs. John Smith.* Ask several male members of the class to react to hypothetical correspondence from their attorney that addresses them as *Mr. Mary Smith.* Ask several married women in the class who have retained their birth names (not changed their last names to their husband's last name) how they react to being called *Mrs. Smith* (husband's last name) rather than *Mary Jones* (woman's birth name).

Option 3    If a feminist jurisprudence class is taught at your school, invite the professor for that course to come in and discuss example of gendered language in the law and the effect it has on both males and females. Be sure that the examples demonstrate stereotyping of both males and females and how it hurts members of both sexes.

Option 4    Invite a rhetorician from the English department of your undergraduate school to come to class to discuss the history and effects of the generic use of *man* or *he.*

Option 5    Invite a female judge or justice to come to class to discuss gender-neutral language in briefs and in the courtroom.

Option 6    To make the point that many words have subtle stereotyping, have the class brainstorm all the terms used for a male parent (*father, dad, daddy, papa, pop, old man*) and ask what the differences are among those terms. You may want to follow by asking the class to make a similar list of the terms for a female parent (*mother, mom, mommy, mama, ma, old lady*). Now ask the class what "neutral" terms we typically use in the law to describe male and female parents. Presumably they will say *father* and *mother.* You can then point out the embedded stereotyping that becomes more apparent in these terms when we use them as verbs. "To father" a child means to procreate; "to mother" a child means to nurture and protect.

## § 6.5 Bias-free Language

<u>Timing:</u>

If one of the memo problems or opinion letter assignments raise the issue of bias-free language, assign this section at that time. If not, assign with section 6.3 and 6.4 when students are drafting or revising their briefs.

<u>General Comments:</u>

Once again, some students in your class may not feel that bias-free language is a serious issue. To make this issue immediately relevant to your class, consider writing into one of your memo or brief assignments an aspect that will naturally raise this issue.

<u>Suggested Teaching Methods:</u>

Option 1    Whenever relevant, point out examples of both biased and bias-free language when they appear in students' sample writing. (Remember to remove students' names from their drafts.)

Option 2    Ask the class to explain what they think is the difference between the terms *American Indian* and *Native American*. Repeat the same point and process with the terms *Mexican American, Chicano/Chicana, Hispanic*, and *Latino/Latina*. *The American Heritage Dictionary of the English Language* 4th edition has good explanations for these terms.

Option 3    Ask the class what are the differences among the terms *non-white, minority*, and *person of color*. Ask the class to consider when they might choose one term over another. (*The American Heritage Dictionary of the English Language* 4th edition has good explanations for these terms.)

## Chapter 7:  Eloquence

General Comments:

If you have a high ability class, the material in this chapter will be appropriate for the whole group.  For average ability groups, you may want to offer workshops on style that are an addition to the regular class.  These workshops can be open to all students, or they can be specifically intended for a smaller select group of high ability students.

## § 7.1  Purple Prose

Timing:

Assign this section to any student whose writing crosses over the line into purple prose.

## § 7.2  Common Features of Eloquent Writing

Option 1    *focus on all features of eloquence*

Select one or two examples of students' writing that contains eloquent passages.  Photocopy or make transparencies or both of those passages.  Read the passages aloud in class.  Ask the students to identify which of the features of eloquence discussed in the chapter the author used.  Which features did the author use that were not discussed in the chapter?

Option 2    *focus on all features of eloquence*

Ask each student to select before class the passage in his or her brief that is the best written.  Makes photocopies or transparencies of several of the selected passages.  Discuss what it is in these passages that the students like.  Ask for recommendations from the class about how they could be further improved.

Option 3    *focus on cadence and stressed and unstressed syllables*

Before class, have students select a passage from their own brief that does not read smoothly when read aloud.  Have the students scan that passage, marking accented and unaccented syllables, to determine if the rhythm is the cause of the awkwardness.  If so, have the students revise the passage, keeping the rhythm in mind.  Make photocopies of three or four examples, showing both the original and the revisions.  Discuss whether the revisions solved the problem.  If not, ask the class to recommend other revisions.

Option 4    *focus on variety in sentence length*

Have students review Section 5.5.  Ask the students to count the number of words in each sentence in 2-3 pages from their drafts of their briefs.  (You may also want them to mark units of meaning.)  They should look at the word counts to see if there is variety in the length of their sentences.  Check too if any short sentences are being used and, if so, if they are being used to highlight important points.  (This option can be done at home or in class.)

Option 5     *focus on parallelism*

Ask students to bring to class examples of parallelism that they deliberately wrote into their briefs.  Make copies of the best examples.  In class, ask students to state what effect they hoped to achieve with the parallelism, and then ask the class whether that effect was achieved.

Option 6     *focus on simile and metaphor*

Point out similes, metaphors, and personification, both fresh versions and cliched versions, when they naturally appear in students' drafts.  Discuss as a class whether a given example is effective.

**Chapter 8:   Grammar**

<u>Timing:</u>

Assign this section on an as needed basis to those students who are having serious writing problems and who cannot apply the information in the other writing sections because they are unfamiliar with basic grammar and its terminology.

## § 8.1  Basic Sentence Grammar

<u>Suggested Teaching Methods:</u>

Students whose writing problems are serious enough to warrant work in this section will almost certainly need to work with their legal writing professor in individualized writing conferences or, if your program has a Writing Advisor or a Writing Specialist, with that person in individualized writing conferences.  In conference, remind students that you are not interested in turning them into grammarians, but rather that you want them to understand enough about the system of language so that they can write effective memos and briefs.  Reassure them that they do not need to have the grammatical terms memorized, although they should be completely comfortable with such terms as *subject, predicate, verb, clause, phrase*, and *pronoun*.  As for other terms such as *gerund, correlative conjunction* and *conjunctive adverb*, their goal should be a general understanding of how these parts of sentences work.

After the student has read the section, you can answer any questions he or she may have about the material, but the focus of subsequent conferences should be that student's own writing.  The section should give the student and legal writing professor a common foundation and terminology to use in future conferences.

## § 8.2  Fragments

<u>Timing:</u>

Assign this section to any student who is writing sentence fragments.

<u>General Comments:</u>

Students who are writing sentence fragments will need special help and will need it immediately.  Encourage them to come in for individual writing conferences either with the legal writing professor or with the Writing Specialist, if your school has one.

<u>Suggested Teaching Method:</u>

If the student is writing only one of the two main types of fragments (missing main verb or subordinate clauses trying to pose as sentences), draw the student's attention to the specific type of fragment he or she is writing.  Some students have an even narrower pattern in their sentence fragments. For example, the only fragments they write may begin with *which* or *although*. If such patterns exist, be sure to point them out to the student so that the student doesn't believe he or she is randomly writing fragments. Such patterns also allow students to develop effective proofreading techniques for fragments. They simply have to search for the word (such as *which* or *although*) and then make sure the "sentence" that follows has a subject and main verb.

Students who have difficulty picking out subjects and verbs can often determine whether something is a fragment or a sentence by reading it aloud to hear if it can "stand alone." Consequently, one proofreading technique for students who write fragments is to have them read their writing aloud, slowly, **with longer than normal pauses after each sentence**. The last point is the significant one: it allows the student to hear when a "sentence" cannot stand alone.

## § 8.3 Verb Tense and Mood

Timing:

Assign this section only as needed to specific students. ESL students may also find Section 10.1.2 helpful.

General Comments:

Students whose first language is not English often have problems with verb tense and thus will need to read this section. Native speakers will generally use verb tense correctly almost without thinking. The two areas that native speakers may need to review are the use of the past perfect tense and the use of the subjunctive mood.

A fair number of law students have difficulty knowing which tense to use for analogous cases. As a general rule, remind students that the facts (defendant *claimed*, plaintiff *moved*) and the actions of the court (court *held*, court *ruled*) were actions that were completed in the past so some form of the past tense is needed. A common law rule derived from a case, however, is on-going, so it is generally written in the present tense.

Example:

To establish title by adverse possession, the person claiming title *must prove* that his or her possession was open, notorious, hostile, exclusive, and under a claim of right for the statutory period.

Examples that demonstrate that the court acted in the past but that the rule continues into the present also help students understand how to use verb tense correctly with analogous cases.

Example:

The court *held* that conduct *is* outrageous when the conduct *is* so extreme in degree as to go beyond all possible bounds of decency.
(past tense *held* for court's past action, but present tense *is* for on-going rule)

Suggested Teaching Method:

Use timelines like those in the section to help students visualize verb tense. Remind them that the "X" on the line that signifies the present is to a large extent a creation of the writer and the context; thus, it may stand for a second or a century, whichever makes sense in this particular case.

## § 8.4  Agreement

General Comments:

Section 8.4.2, Pronoun-Antecedent Agreement, fits nicely with Section 6.4, Gender-Neutral Language, because some misguided efforts to correct gendered language end up in pronoun agreement problems. Another option is to assign Section 8.4.2 with Section 8.5 and treat all the issues that relate to pronouns together.

Suggested Teaching Method:

Most students with subject-verb agreement problems have these problems because there are several words separating the subject and verb. Consequently, their ear hears one of the intervening words and matches the verb to the intervening word and not to the subject. To prevent this problem, have students first identify the verb in the sentence and then the subject. Then have them read the two together without any of the intervening words. Most native speakers will "hear" when they have the correct form of the verb. Note that students who have trouble picking out the subject and verb in a sentence are far more successful if you ask them to select the verb first, reminding them that the verb is the part of the sentence that changes when the timeframe change.

## § 8.5  Pronoun Reference

General Comments:

Because most legal writing students have some problems with pronoun reference, the entire class should read this section. Sections 8.5.1 and 8.5.2 are far more important that 8.5.3, which is more of a grammatical technicality. In Section 8.5.1, help student to see that careless use of pronouns can lead to dramatically different interpretations by different readers. In Section 8.5.2, help students to see that broad pronoun reference is more than a grammatical problem; pinning down exactly what those pronouns are substitutes for requires discipline and control over the content.

<u>Suggested Teaching Method:</u>

After the students have read the section, give them sample sentences, preferably in context, with ambiguous pronouns. (Examples can be found in the *The Legal Writing Handbook, Practice Book* published by Aspen Law & Business or ideally in the students' own writing. See, for example *United States v. Bass*, 490 F.2d 846 (1974) for a case that involved an ambiguous pronoun.) Ask for possible interpretations. Have the students practice revising the sentences so that they are not ambiguous. Repeat the same process with sample sentences that have a broad pronoun reference problem.

## § 8.6 Modifiers

<u>General Comments:</u>

Few law students have thought much about the potential ambiguities created by carelessly used modifiers. Most have heard the terms *dangling modifier* or *dangling participle*, but few know what they mean. This section should be used to raise their level of awareness about modifiers and their potential problems.

<u>Suggested Teaching Method:</u>

Select a sentence from a student's writing and demonstrate how the meaning changes if a modifier such an *only*, *merely*, or *simply* is moved to different slots in the sentence.

For comic relief, show students examples of dangling modifiers that yield ludicrous results.

Example:

> Crumpled behind a filing cabinet, Mr. Smith found the missing file.

## § 8.7 Parallelism

<u>Timing:</u>

This section of the book should be assigned when students are writing issue statements. It is also relevant when students need to write lists of elements or factors, so you may want to refer back to it when students are writing rule sections. Parallelism should also be reviewed when students are working on persuasive writing techniques.

<u>General Comments:</u>

A surprisingly high percentage of law students seem to be unfamiliar with the concept of parallelism. Consequently, this is one of the few grammar chapters that you will probably have to assign to the whole class and discuss during class.

<u>Suggested Teaching Method:</u>

For many students, it is easier to see and understand how the parallelism should work if you draw a diagram similar to the one below on the board.

| (introduction) | when_____ |
| | when_____ ,and/but |
| | when_____ |

Remind students that each "when" clause (or item in the parallelism) should read smoothly off of the introductory portion of the sentence.

## Chapter 9: Punctuation

## § 9.1 The Comma

<u>Timing:</u>

Whenever possible, teach punctuation in context and at the points in the writing process (revising and editing) when students should be concerned about surface features such as punctuation. In many legal writing programs, class time is so limited that little if any time can be devoted to punctuation problems. For this reason, many programs use additional workshops or special sessions to provide instruction in punctuation.

<u>General Comments:</u>

Many law students punctuate by "feel"; that is, they add punctuation when they have a sense that they should but without knowing exactly why. Others use the "pause method"; that is, they add punctuation, particularly commas, whenever they want the reader to pause.

Both methods are somewhat satisfactory in some cases, but they have some obvious shortcomings. The "feel" method assumes that the writer has absorbed all the rules and applies them intuitively. The "pause" method assumes that readers pause only at punctuation and that all of the sentence's ebb and flow is controlled by punctuation. Both assumptions are risky, often foolhardy, and sometimes wrong.

While we do not offer a rule for every given punctuation question, we do recommend that law students should assume a rule exists for a situation in which they are in doubt about the correct punctuation and that when in doubt, they should look it up.

<u>Suggested Teaching Method:</u>

Punctuation, particularly commas, is best taught in context. When you observe that a comma rule is being broken by a substantial number of your students, use examples from your current writing assignment to demonstrate the correct punctuation.

When critiquing drafts and final papers, comment on recurring punctuation errors and refer the student to the appropriate rule in this chapter.

<u>Quick Tips to Teaching Commas:</u>

*Rule 1*

Impress upon students that memorizing the seven coordinating conjunctions is time efficient because certain rules apply with other types of connectors in much larger, unwieldy groups.  An easy mnemonic device for remembering the coordinating conjunctions is FANBOYS:  F=for, A=and, N=nor, B=but, O=or, Y=yet, S=so.

*Rule 4*

Students have more difficulty with this punctuation rule than any other.  Fortunately, though, the errors related to this rule are almost all the same:  the student uses *which* when the situation requires *that*, possibly because *which* sounds more formal and therefore more like legal writing.  Because the errors fall into this pattern, students can check their writing by simply looking for instances where they have used *which* but not put a comma before it.  More often than not, those uses of *which* should be changed to *that*.

*Rule 8*

This rule can be reduced to the following:

Periods & commas→go inside
Colons & semicolons→go outside
Everything else→it depends

## § 9.2 The Semicolon

General Comments:

Because there seems to be some kind of "semicolon mystique," many writers try to avoid using them altogether.  This response leaves them with one less useful tool for controlling the longer sentences typical of legal writing.  It is also an unnecessary response to a punctuation mark that is easy to master.

Suggested Teaching Method:

Remind students of the following chart for a sentence with a semicolon

_____ ; _____.
(could be a sentence)                    (could be a sentence)

Remind them that everything before the semicolon should be able to stand alone as a sentence; remind them that everything after the semicolon should also be able to stand alone as a sentence.  (Some students have a bit of difficulty with the preceding tip when the second main clause uses a pronoun for a subject.  You may need to remind them that pronouns like *it* and *he* can be the subject of sentences and still correctly refer back to a preceding sentence for their antecedent.)

## § 9.3  The Colon

Timing:

Assign this section in conjunction with § 9.5.1, § 9.5.2, and § 9.5.3 on the appropriate use of quotations, quotation marks, ellipses, and brackets.  Refer back to this section when the students begin persuasive writing, but at that point focus on the use of colons to set up explanations and elaborations.

## § 9.4  The Apostrophe

General Comments:

Point out to students that one of the most common errors with apostrophes is to use the plural instead of the possessive.  The error occurs most often when the noun that needs to be possessive is inanimate or an abstraction.

## § 9.5  Other Marks of Punctuation

Timing:

Assign in conjunction with § 9.3 on colons and § 6.2.3 on the excessive use of quotations in legal writing.

## § 9.6  Comma Splices and Fused Sentences

General Comments:

Refer students to Rule 1 in the comma section (§ 9.1) and if necessary to section 8.1 on Basic Sentence Grammar.

## Chapter 10:  Legal Writing for English-as-a-Second-Language Students

Timing:

Because it may be difficult for you to determine whether or not a given student is an ESL law student and because you may risk offending or embarrassing a given student if you ask him or her whether English is his or her first language, the best approach may be to point out Chapter 10 to the entire class at the beginning of the course and simply say that it is recommended reading for all ESL students.

As the course progresses, some ESL students may identify themselves to you and ask for help with specific problems in their writing. You may then want to refer these students again to the sections that address specific problems.

General Comments:

We begin with the assumption that ESL law students intending to practice law in the United States[2] will want their writing to conform not only to the grammatical rules and standard use of English but also to the rhetorical preferences of the U.S. legal culture. Others might argue that the traditions of writing about law in English would be enriched if ESL law students wrote using the rhetorical preferences they bring from other cultures. We will leave that debate to another forum.

We also assume that it is probably impossible and almost certainly unnecessary for legal writing professors to know all the rhetorical preferences of the native cultures of their ESL law students. Nevertheless, a general awareness of why many ESL law students make the choices they do should lead to improved communication between legal writing professors and ESL law students and to more effective teaching of these students. Furthermore, encouraging ESL law students to reflect on what they know about writing in their native cultures should help those students appreciate the traditions they come from and assist them in making the adjustments in their writing in English that they will inevitably need to make.

What we think legal writing professors do need to be fully aware of are the underlying rhetorical conventions and preferences in writing in the U.S. culture. With conscious knowledge of these culturally-bound conventions and preferences, legal writing professors can give their ESL law students more useful advice and facilitate these students' cross-cultural transition.

In many cases, advice about teaching ESL law students mirrors good advice about teaching any law student. Perhaps the only difference is that the professor needs to

---

[2] Obviously some ESL students attending U.S. law schools intend to return to their native countries. Unless these students foresee an ongoing need to write about law in English, they may not find it time efficient to attempt to develop the highest levels of fluency discussed in this chapter.

remember that many ESL law students have considerably less shared cultural knowledge with the professor than do native-speaking law students. Consequently, it is even more imperative to give complete explanations and not take it for granted that all students understand the same instructions, advice, and assignments in the same way.

For example, when giving a legal writing assignment to ESL law students, try to give as much information as you can about the context in which the piece of writing would occur had it been assigned to a practicing attorney. Talk extensively about who reads such a document, what that reader is like, what that reader's purposes are, and what the writer's purposes are. Remember that judges, lawyers, clients, police officers, etc. are viewed very differently from culture to culture and that without the extra explanation, an ESL law student may be making some assumptions that are not true in this culture. Provide as many good examples of similar types of writing as you can so that the students can see what registers of language are appropriate and how other writers have negotiated similar writing problems. Do not be surprised, however, if some of your ESL law students closely imitate models you give them; imitation is common and acceptable for student writers in many cultures. We recommend that you give explicit instructions about how you want students to learn from and use good examples of writing that you share with them.

If you are giving an exam, avoid using slang in the hypothetical. Because ESL students won't have an opportunity to look up a slang phrase used in an exam, they may either misunderstand part of the exam or simply worry needlessly that they are missing something important.

Be aware that some teaching strategies that work well with native speakers may be ineffective with ESL law students (and vice versa). For example, using free writing as a heuristic strategy will probably be ineffective with most ESL law students. In many cultures, writing to discover one's ideas is not an opinion. Reading writing aloud may also not be an effective strategy for non-native speakers. In fact, an explanation based on formal grammar rules, which may not be the best teaching technique for native speakers of English, may often be the most effective teaching technique for those ESL law students who learned English from teachers using a traditional grammar-based method.

If your legal writing program has students who work as teaching assistants or as tutors who meet with students to discuss their writing, you may find that ESL law students have somewhat different notions about the TA's or tutor's role. They may assume that only the legal writing professor can talk about the larger issues related to writing such as clarity and organization and that the TA or tutor is there to show them how to fix mistakes and correct minor errors. (Admittedly, many native-speaking law students also mistakenly believe that tutorials are editing services.) Many ESL law students are extremely hesitant to ask their legal writing professors questions, so they may assume that the role of the T A or writing tutor is to answer their questions. Not surprisingly, then, there can be a great deal of misunderstanding and miscommunication when ESL law students have writing conferences with TA ' s and writing tutors who have been taught to work on higher order concerns before sentence-level corrections and who have been instructed to ask questions and keep the responsibility for the writing with the author. Having come from cultures where students are expected to listen and take notes, ESL law students may not realize that they are expected to take a more interactive role in writing conferences. Obviously, one solution is clear explanations of how the TA or writing tutor works with students and what to expect from a writing conference. Judith Kilborn[2] also suggests that simple changes like rephrasing a "why" or "how" question with a "please explain..." beginning may help ESL writers in writing conferences. Because many ESL students feel quite nervous about writing conferences--whether the conference is with a TA, tutor, or the legal writing professor -- some casual conversation at the beginning of the conference may help put the student at ease.

Beware of advising ESL law students not to think about or write about the law and their legal writing assignments in their native languages. There is some research indicating that ESL writers may use this technique to their advantage.

Most ESL law students will want as much information as you can give them about rhetorical preferences including such things as suitable levels of formality, preferred sentence length, acceptability of using first and second person, the amount of passive voice and metaphorical language that is typical, but be careful to relay to them what you see as the *range* of what is acceptable. In addition, because many other cultures have quite different notions of coherence than does the U.S. culture, you will probably want to spend extra time with your ESL students emphasizing cohesive devices in English (see Section 3.2.2).

A few ESL law students will ask or even expect that you mark and correct every error in their writing. For some ESL students, this might become a daunting task for both student and teacher. Alternatives to this approach include focusing on just those errors that you and other legal readers would find most distracting, looking for patterns in the errors and focusing on one or two types of error at a time, or advising the student to work with a writing advisor or specialist (if one is available at your school) on the ESL related problems.

In any case, generalizations about ESL law students are inherently misleading because of the great diversity in the ESL law student population. For some students, even the term ESL is misleading because English is not their second language; it is their third, fourth fifth or even sixth language. ESL law students will also differ by culture, by educational background, by the type of language training they had, by the age when they began learning English, and by how experienced they are as writers in their native languages. All of these factors, as well as individual intellectual ability, cognitive style, and personality traits, will affect how they handle writing in English about law.

---

[2] Muriel Harris, *Cultural Conflicts in the Writing Center: Expectations and Assumptions of ESL Students* in Writing in Multicultural Settings, Severino and others, eds. (1997).

Recognizing their differences, we can still anticipate some of problems that many ESL law students will have in legal writing. In addition to the grammatical and rhetorical challenges discussed in the student text, ESL law students typically struggle mightily with word choice. Connotations and nuances make it more difficult for ESL law students to be effective advocates. Students who have had extensive exposure to textbook/academic English or to street English but not to the other tend to have difficulty selecting the appropriate register of language.

Lack of vocabulary and fear of choosing words incorrectly add yet another composing problem: a disrupted flow in their ideas. The simple reality for ESL law students is that it takes them considerably longer to produce the same number of words as it does a native speaker.

Well-founded concern about word choice sometimes leads ESL law students to a third problem: over-reliance on quoting or copying without attribution. Be sure to explain exactly what you and the U.S. legal culture consider to be plagiarism. ESL law students, and for that matter many native speakers of English, have widely different points of view about what is the appropriate way to use and credit the words and ideas of another. Know too that in many other cultures there is a much stronger cultural taboo against refusing a request for help than we have in the United States. Consequently, unless this cultural difference is explained to ESL law students, they may follow their native culture's approved mores of helping others without realizing the drastic consequences such help may have on their law school careers.

Finally, some, but not all, ESL law students are relatively isolated from the rest of the student body. This is unfortunate on several levels. Not only are many of these students struggling with loneliness, their isolation also gives them fewer opportunities to hear and use English. For these reasons, some legal writing professors make an extra effort to have office conferences with their ESL law students, and some have helped these students find study groups where they can practice expressing their analysis and arguments in English.

In conclusion, we want to raise what is probably the ultimate question for ESL law students arid their legal writing professors: how good must their writing be? Do they have to be about to pass for native speakers/writers? Does their writing in English only have to be good enough to be understood? Is it realistic to strive to eliminate all errors, or should we be satisfied if the writing is free of jarring errors? We don't have the answers for these questions. We raise them here because we know that ultimately these are the issues that each of us must address as we teach, and evaluate, English-as-a-second-language law students.
Bibliography for legal writing professors teaching ESL law students

For an extensive discussion of the iddues relevant to ESL students and their writing

Ilona Leki, Understanding ESL Writers: A Guide for Teachers (1992).

Writings in Multicultural Settings 198-244 (Carol Severino et al. eds., 1997) (contains four invaluable articles, which include an overview of contrastive rhetoric's insights into ESL writing, advice about the learning and writing processes of ESL students, and a thoughtful discussion about the limitations of contrastive rhetoric and some of the problems with its methodologies. )

For a discussion of the philosophical underpinnings of second language writing instruction and considerations for writing instruction

Second Language Writing: Research Insights for the Classroom (Barbara Kroll, ed., 1990).

For a discussion of the connection between culture and logic

Jill J. Ramsfield, Is "Logic" Culturally Based? A Contrastive, International Approach to the U.S. Law Classroom, 47 J. Legal Educ.157 (1997).

For an excellent dictionary for sophisticated ESL students

Longman Dictionary of Contemporary English, (3d ed., 1995).


For an ESL grammar book that discusses issues not included in this chapter, including relative clauses. noun clauses. adjective and adverb clauses. and word order

Janet Lange & Ellen Lange, Writing Clearly: An Editing Guide (1993).

Allen Ascher, Think About Editing: A Grammar Editing Guide for ESL Writers (1993).

For an overview of how people learn second languages

Susan M. Gass & Larry Selinker, Second Language Acquisition: An Introductory Course (1994).

For a discussion about ESL students in writing centers

Muriel Harris, Cultural Conflicts in the Writing Center: Expectations & Assumptions of ESL Students in Writing in Multicultural Settings (Carol Severino et al., eds., 1997).

For background on contrastive rhetoric

Robert B. Kaplan, Contrastive Rhetoric & Second Language Learning: Notes Toward a Theory of Contrastive Rhetoric in Writing Across Languages & Cultures: Issues in Contrastive Rhetoric 275 (Alan C. Purves ed. 1988).

## For information on the Bolinger principle

Dwight Bolinger, *Entailment & the Meaning of Structures,* 2 Glossa 119 (1968). (In a later experiment testing whether the Bolinger principle was an effective way to teach which verbs require gerunds and infinitives, the results showed that the experimental group who had been taught the Bolinger principle did "significantly better on the discrete point tests." *See* Juliet Rosemarie Vawser , *An Experiment Testing the Bolinger Principle to Teach Gerunds & Infinitives,* Master of Arts in English: TESOL Thesis, February 22, 1988.

Nguyen Van So, The Semantic Interpretation of Infinitives & Gerunds as Sentential Complements, (unpublished M. TESL thesis, UCLA).

## For more information about reader-responsible and writer-responsible languages

John Hinds, *Reader Versus Writer Responsibility: A New Typology* in Writing Across Languages: Analysis of L2 text, (U. Connor & R. Kaplan eds. 1987).

## Other useful resources

Donna M. Johnson & Duane H. Roen, Richness in Writing: Empowering ESL Students, (1989).

Professor Jill Ramsfield, Director of Legal Writing, Georgetown Law School, has also published a bibliography for legal writing professors teaching ESL law students.